GRAPHIC LIBRARY

GRAPHIC HISTORY

THE BATTLE OF
GETTYSBURG

by Michael Burgan

illustrated by Steve Erwin, Keith Williams,
and Charles Barnett III

Consultant:
James M. McPherson
Professor of History
Princeton University
Princeton, New Jersey

Capstone
press

Mankato, Minnesota

Graphic Library is published by Capstone Press,
151 Good Counsel Drive, P.O. Box 669, Mankato, Minnesota 56002.
www.capstonepress.com

Printed in the United States of America in Stevens Point, Wisconsin.
122009
005644R

Library of Congress Cataloging-in-Publication Data
Burgan, Michael.
    The battle of Gettysburg / by Michael Burgan; illustrated by Steve Erwin, Keith Williams,
and Charles Barnett III.
        p. cm.—(Graphic library. Graphic history)
    Summary: "In graphic novel format, tells the story of the Battle of Gettysburg, the three-day
battle that was the turning point in the Civil War"—Provided by publisher.
    Includes bibliographical references and index.
    ISBN-13: 978-0-7368-5491-7 (hardcover)
    ISBN-10: 0-7368-5491-6 (hardcover)
    ISBN-13: 978-0-7368-6880-8 (softcover pbk.)
    ISBN-10: 0-7368-6880-1 (softcover pbk.)
    1. Gettysburg, Battle of, Gettysburg, Pa., 1863—Juvenile literature. I. Erwin, Steve, ill.
II. Williams, Keith, 1958 Feb. 24– ill. III. Barnett, Charles, III, ill. IV. Title. V. Series.
E475.53.B965 2006
973.7'349—dc22   2005025380

Art Direction and Design
Bob Lentz

Production Artist
Alison Thiele

Colorist
Benjamin Hunzeker

Editor
Christine Peterson

Map on page 8 courtesy of the Geography and Map Division, Library of Congress.

Editor's note: Direct quotations from primary sources are indicated by a yellow background.

Direct quotations appear on the following pages:
Page 18, from General James Longstreet's account of the Battle of Gettysburg as published in
    the *Philadelphia Times* November 1876 (www.swcivilwar.com/LongstreetGettys1stPhilArti
    cle.html).
Page 19, from George Pickett's letter dated July 4, 1863, as published in *Heart of a Soldier: As
    Revealed in the Intimate Letters of General George E. Pickett* (New York: S. Moyle, 1913).
Pages 20, 22, from *The Story of a Confederate Boy in the Civil War* by Virginia Infantryman
    David Emmons Johnston (Portland, Ore.: Glass & Prudhomme, 1914).
Page 23, from an article by Confederate Captain Robert A. Bright, originally published
    February 7, 1904, in the Richmond, Virginia, *Times-Dispatch*, and recorded in the Southern
    Historical Society Papers (http://docsouth.unc.edu/pickett/pickett.html#pick91).
Page 25, from a conversation between Abraham Lincoln and his secretary John Hay on
    July 14, 1863, as recorded in *Inside Lincoln's White House: The Complete Civil War Diary
    of John Hay* (Carbondale, Ill.: Southern Illinois University Press, 1997).
Pages 26, 29, from Abraham Lincoln's Gettysburg Address at the Library of Congress
    (http://www.loc.gov/exhibits/gadd/gadrft.html).

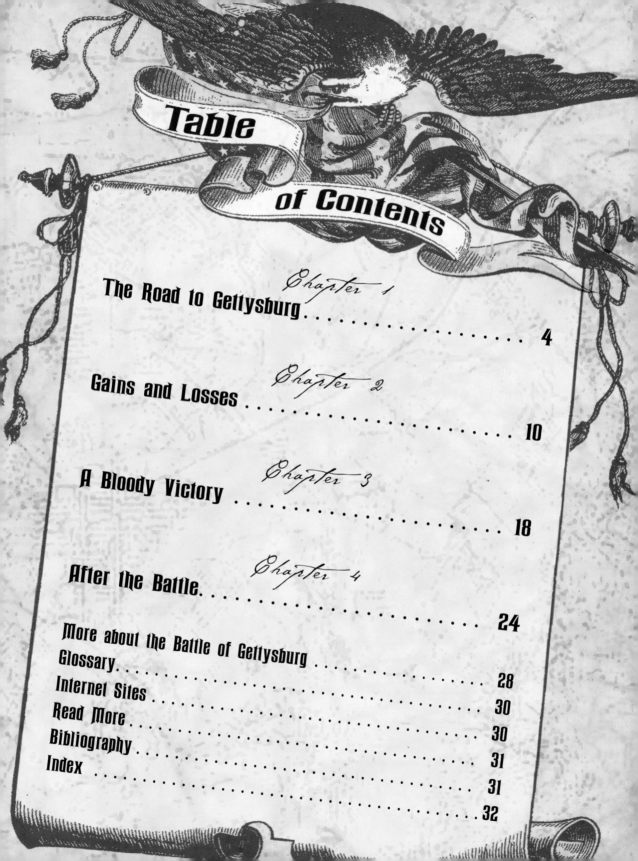

Table of Contents

CHAPTER 1
The Road to Gettysburg

In November 1860, American voters chose the 16th president of the United States. To most people, slavery was the most important issue of the day. Southern states allowed slavery, while northern states did not. Americans had sharply different views on slavery.

VOTE

HONEST ABE LINCOLN

VOTE FOR

DOUGLAS

I'm for Abraham Lincoln. He'll stop slavery from spreading into new states and territories.

VOTE HERE

I'll vote for Lincoln, but I say we should get rid of slavery once and for all.

Stephen Douglas is my man. He says the territories should decide for themselves if they want slavery.

Lincoln defeated Douglas and three other men to win the presidency. Southern states feared that Lincoln would try to end slavery.

CHAPTER 2

Gains and Losses

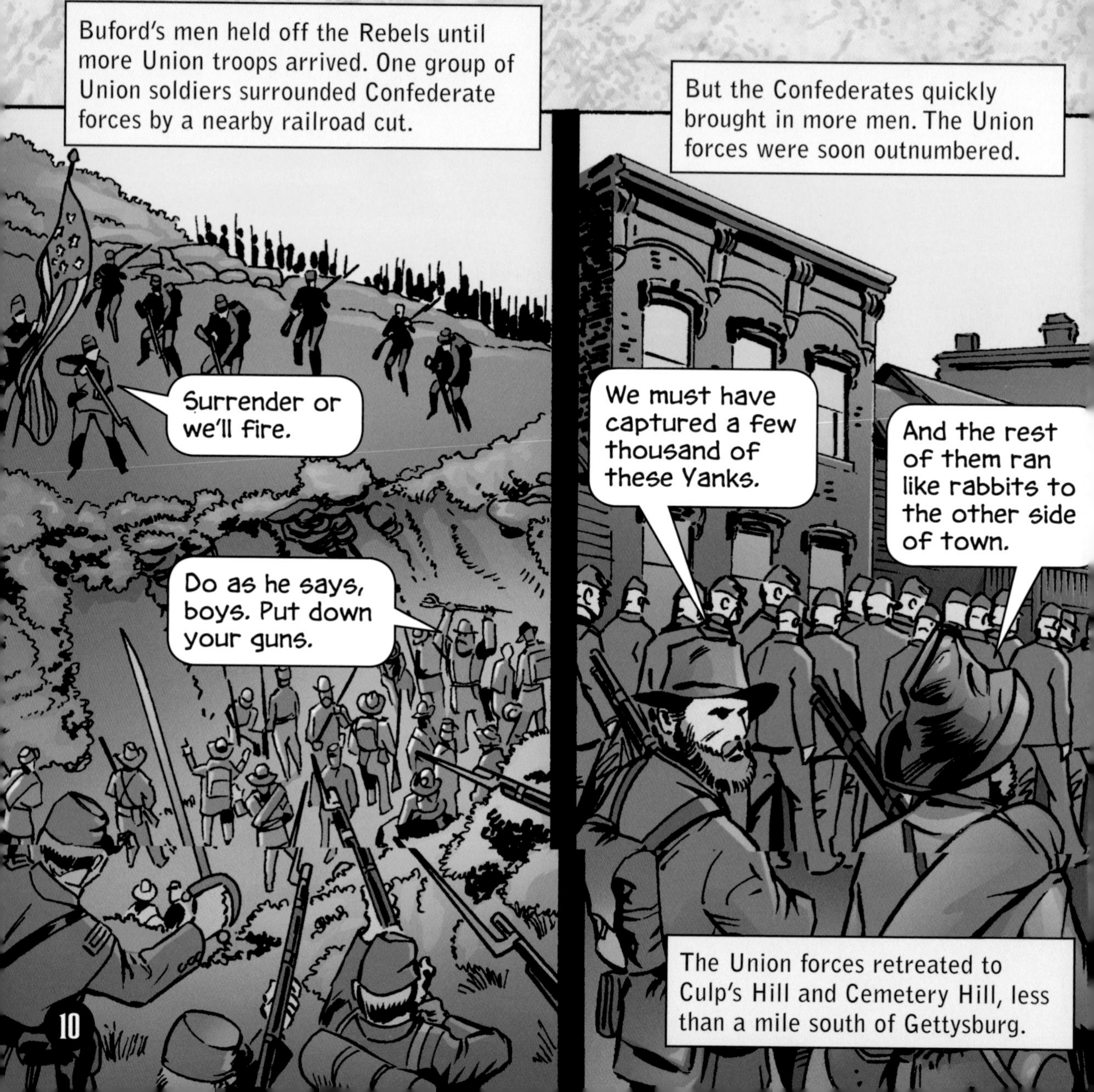
Buford's men held off the Rebels until more Union troops arrived. One group of Union soldiers surrounded Confederate forces by a nearby railroad cut.
Surrender or we'll fire.
Do as he says, boys. Put down your guns.
But the Confederates quickly brought in more men. The Union forces were soon outnumbered.
We must have captured a few thousand of these Yanks.
And the rest of them ran like rabbits to the other side of town.
The Union forces retreated to Culp's Hill and Cemetery Hill, less than a mile south of Gettysburg.

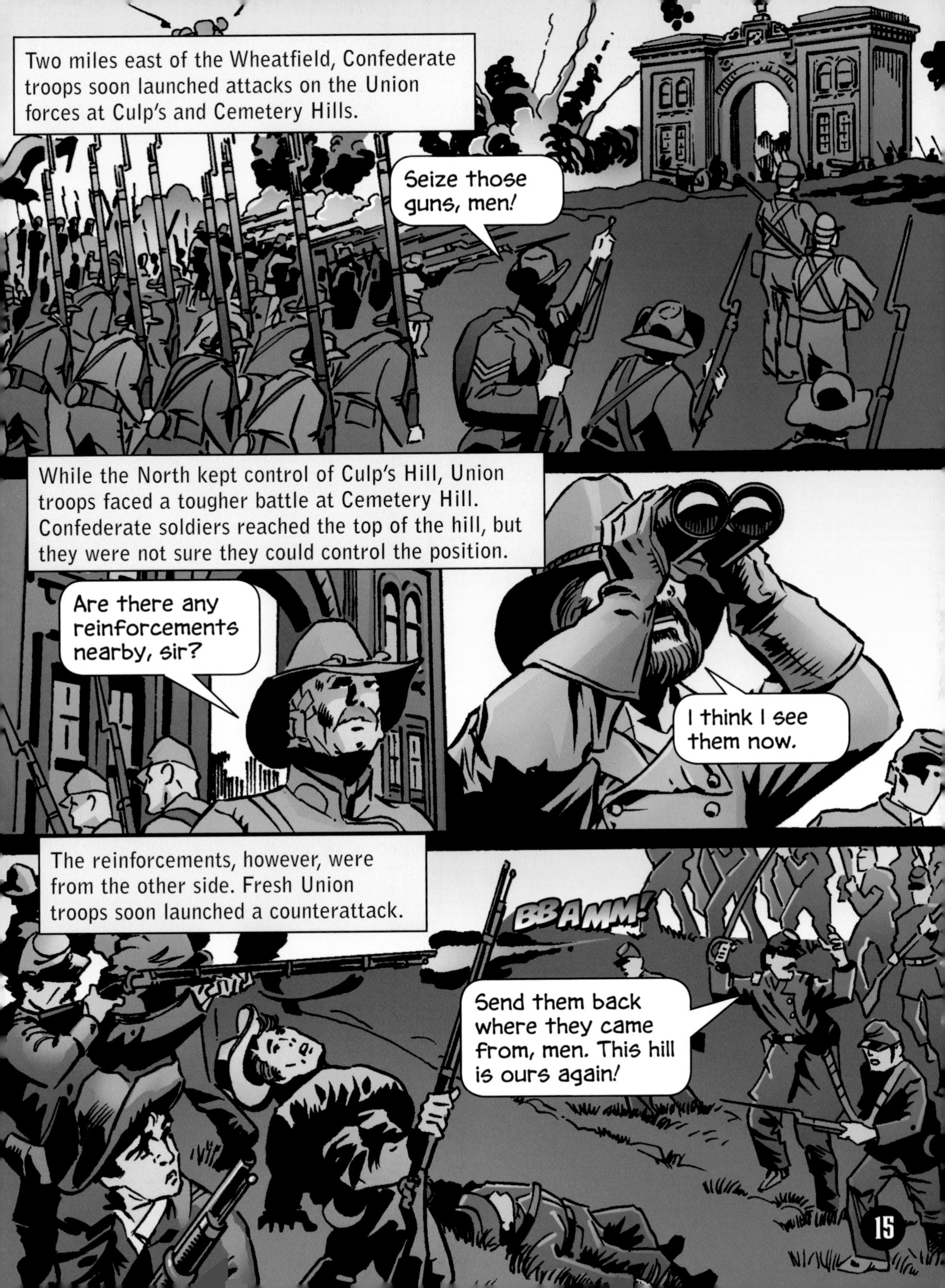
Two miles east of the Wheatfield, Confederate troops soon launched attacks on the Union forces at Culp's and Cemetery Hills.
Seize those guns, men!
While the North kept control of Culp's Hill, Union troops faced a tougher battle at Cemetery Hill. Confederate soldiers reached the top of the hill, but they were not sure they could control the position.
Are there any reinforcements nearby, sir?
I think I see them now.
The reinforcements, however, were from the other side. Fresh Union troops soon launched a counterattack.
BBAMM!
Send them back where they came from, men. This hill is ours again!

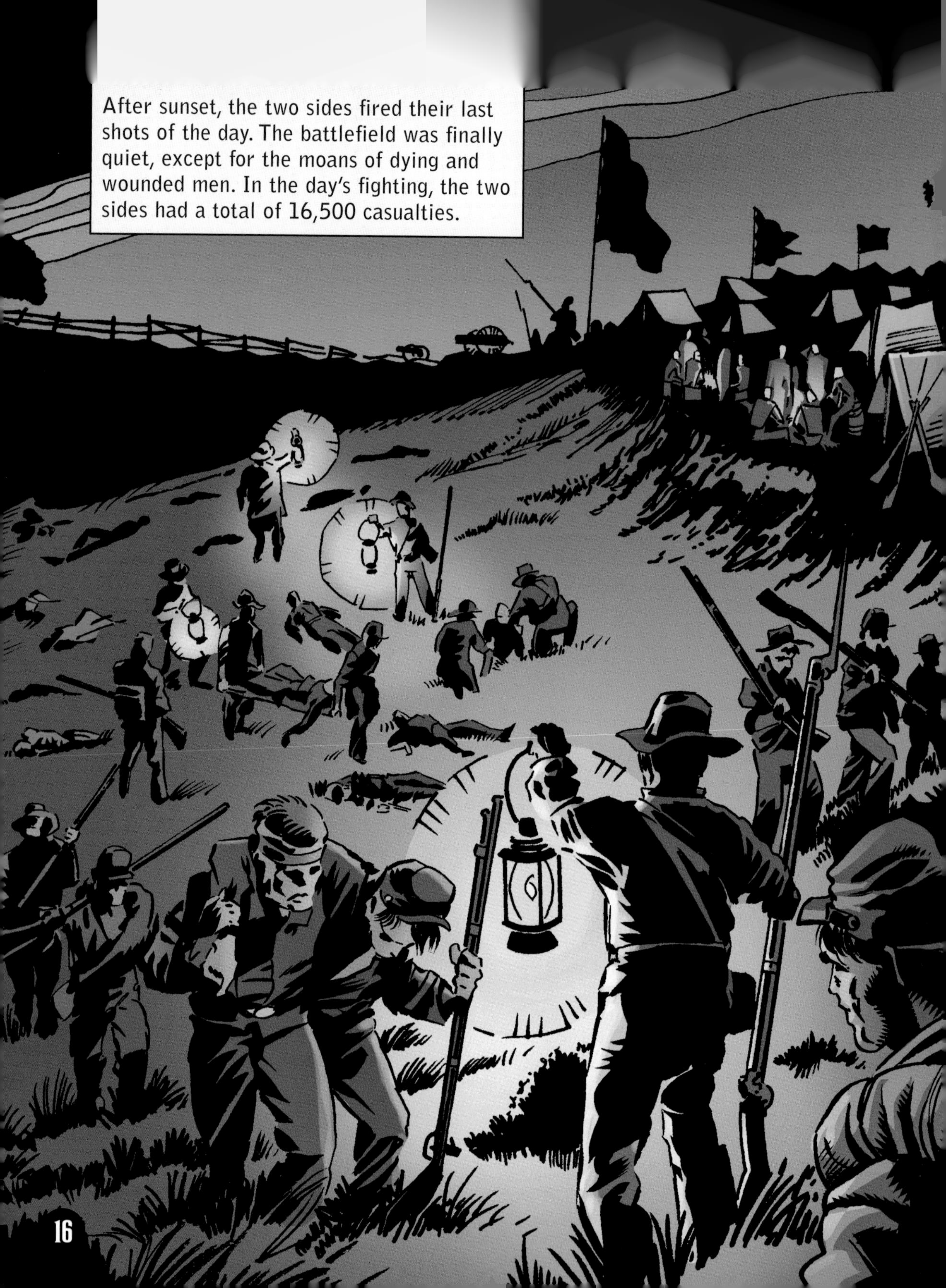
After sunset, the two sides fired their last shots of the day. The battlefield was finally quiet, except for the moans of dying and wounded men. In the day's fighting, the two sides had a total of 16,500 casualties.

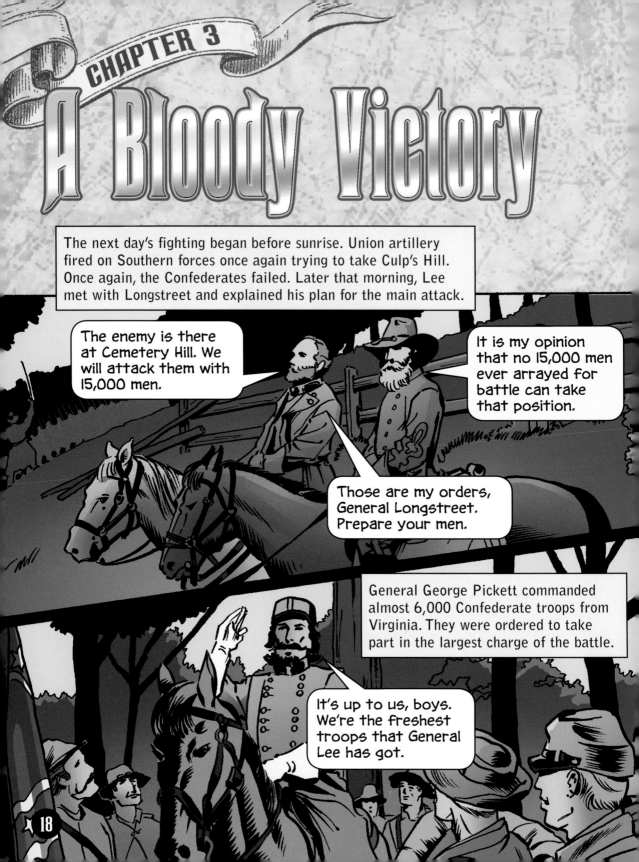

CHAPTER 3
A Bloody Victory

The next day's fighting began before sunrise. Union artillery fired on Southern forces once again trying to take Culp's Hill. Once again, the Confederates failed. Later that morning, Lee met with Longstreet and explained his plan for the main attack.

The enemy is there at Cemetery Hill. We will attack them with 15,000 men.

It is my opinion that no 15,000 men ever arrayed for battle can take that position.

Those are my orders, General Longstreet. Prepare your men.

General George Pickett commanded almost 6,000 Confederate troops from Virginia. They were ordered to take part in the largest charge of the battle.

It's up to us, boys. We're the freshest troops that General Lee has got.

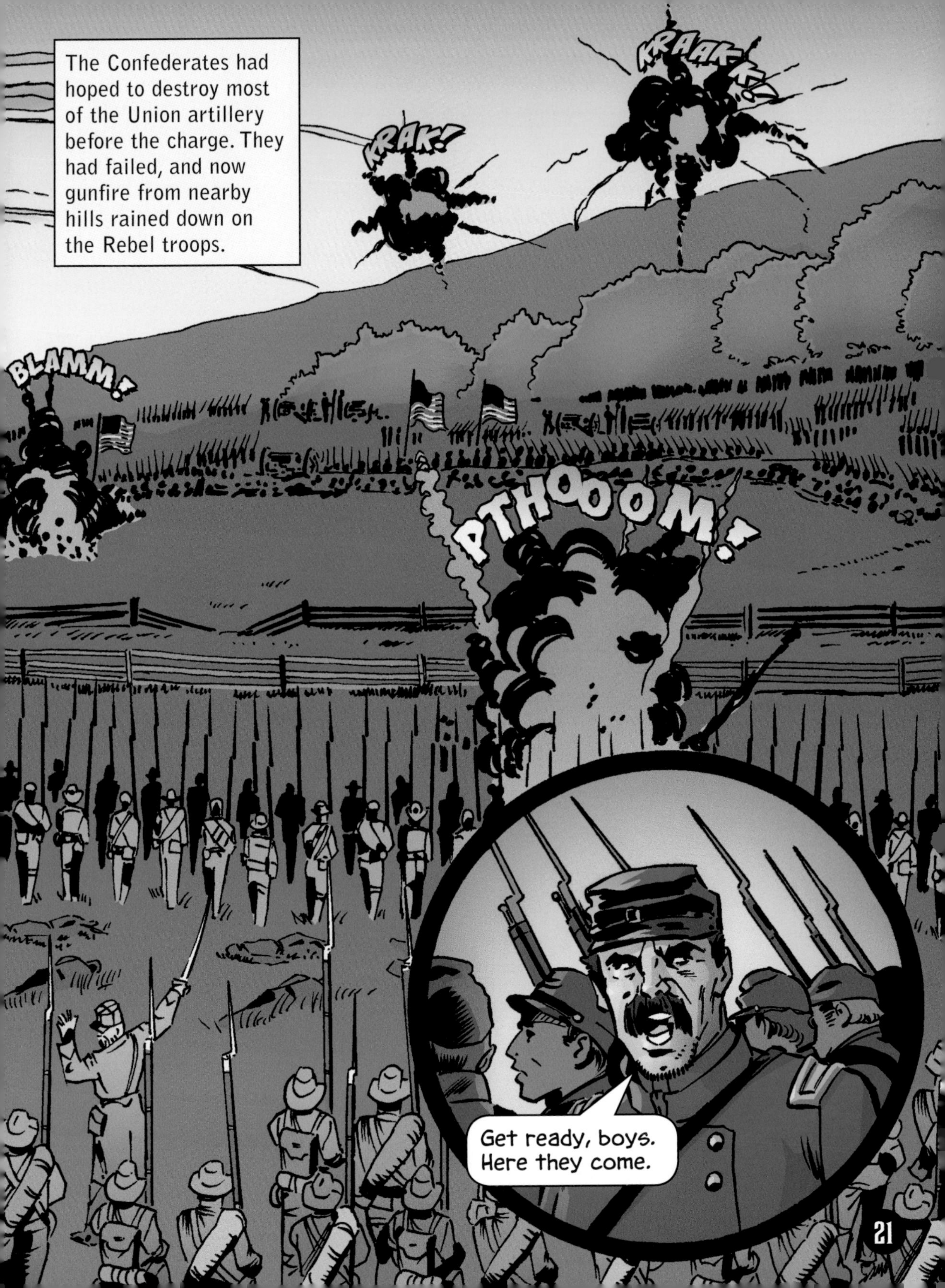
The Confederates had hoped to destroy most of the Union artillery before the charge. They had failed, and now gunfire from nearby hills rained down on the Rebel troops.
KRAK!
KRAAKK!
BLAMM!
PTHOOOM!
Get ready, boys. Here they come.

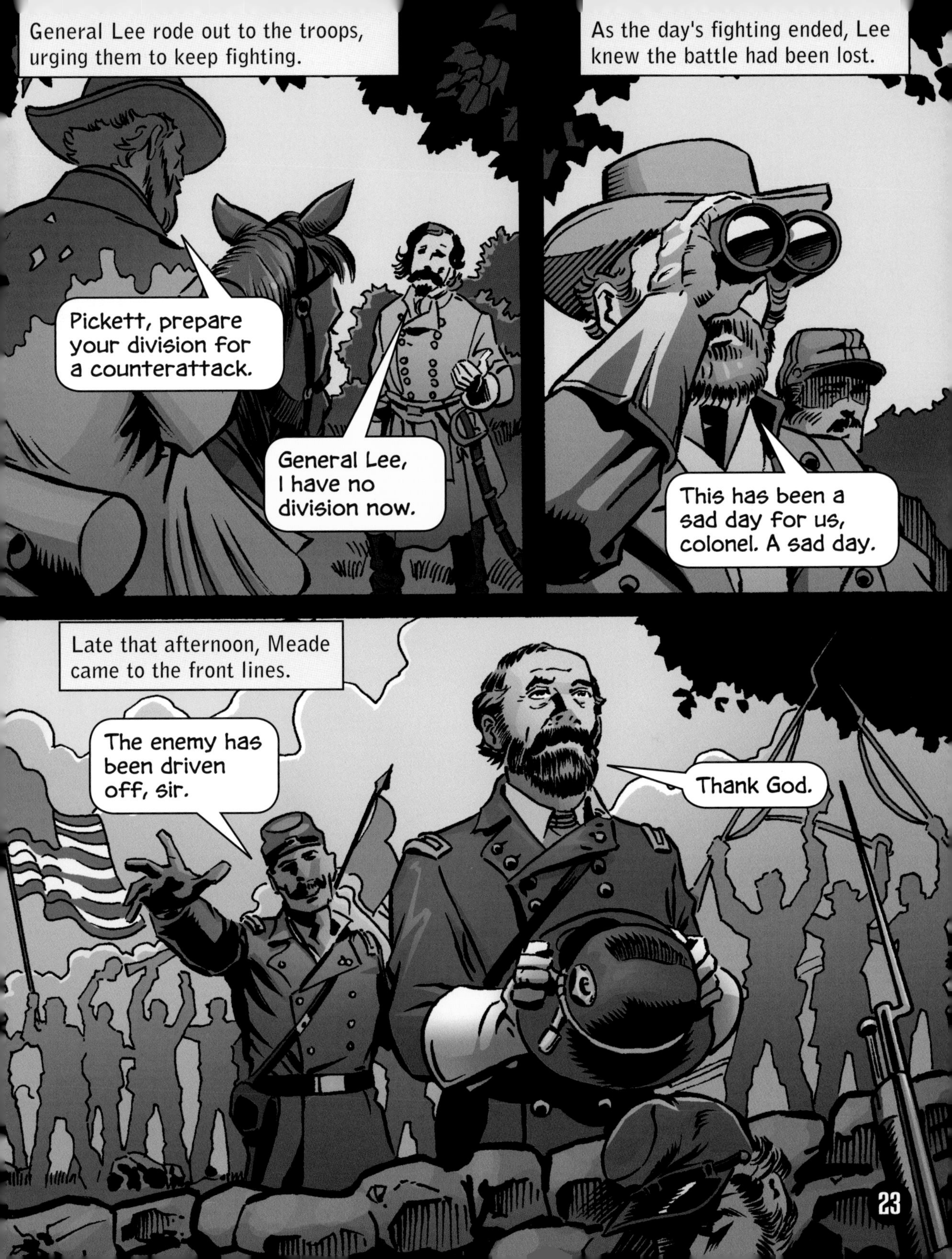
General Lee rode out to the troops, urging them to keep fighting.
Pickett, prepare your division for a counterattack.
General Lee, I have no division now.
As the day's fighting ended, Lee knew the battle had been lost.
This has been a sad day for us, colonel. A sad day.
Late that afternoon, Meade came to the front lines.
The enemy has been driven off, sir.
Thank God.

CHAPTER 4

After the Battle

The next morning, Lee began to pull his troops out of Gettysburg. A train of wagons 17 miles long headed west, away from the battlefield.

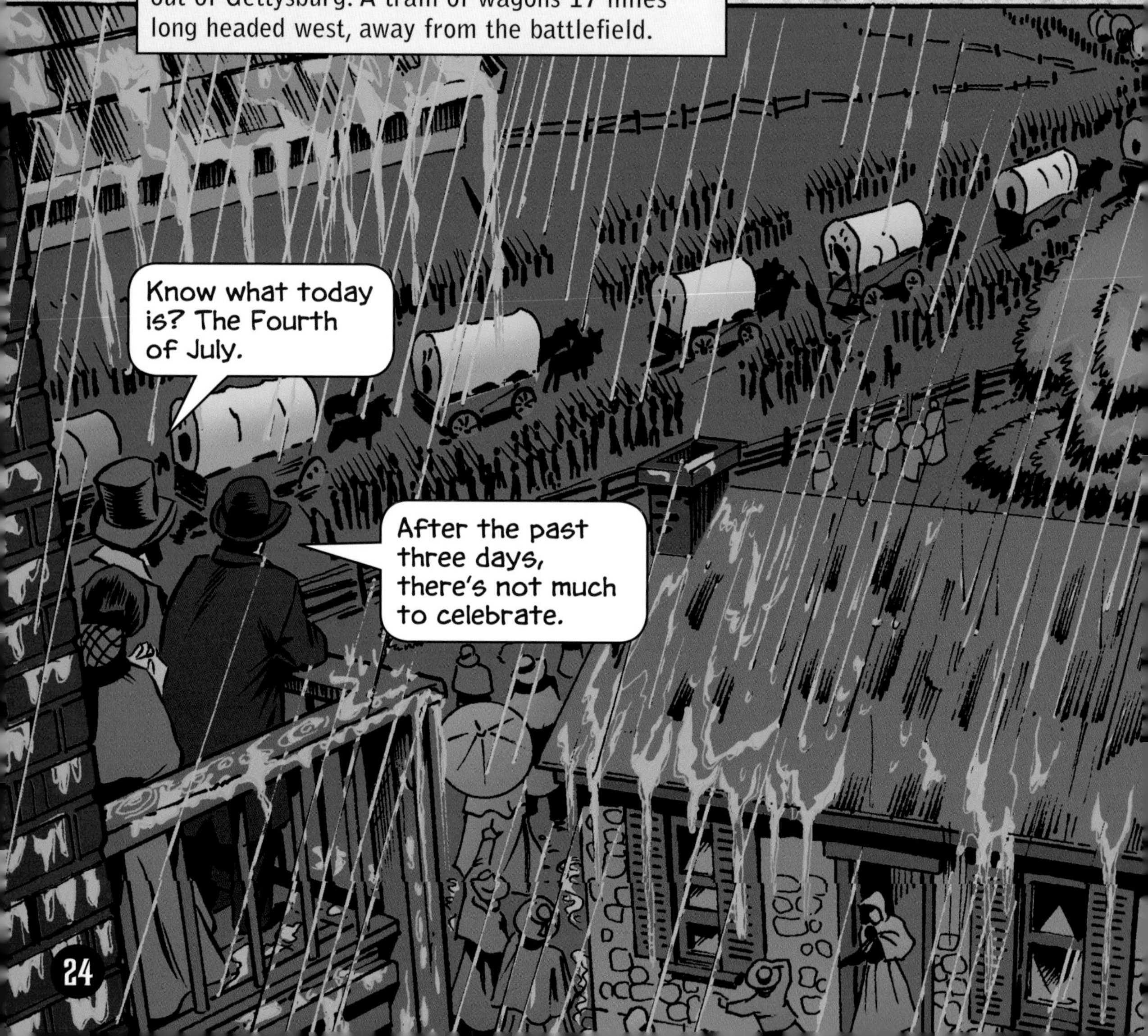

Know what today is? The Fourth of July.
After the past three days, there's not much to celebrate.

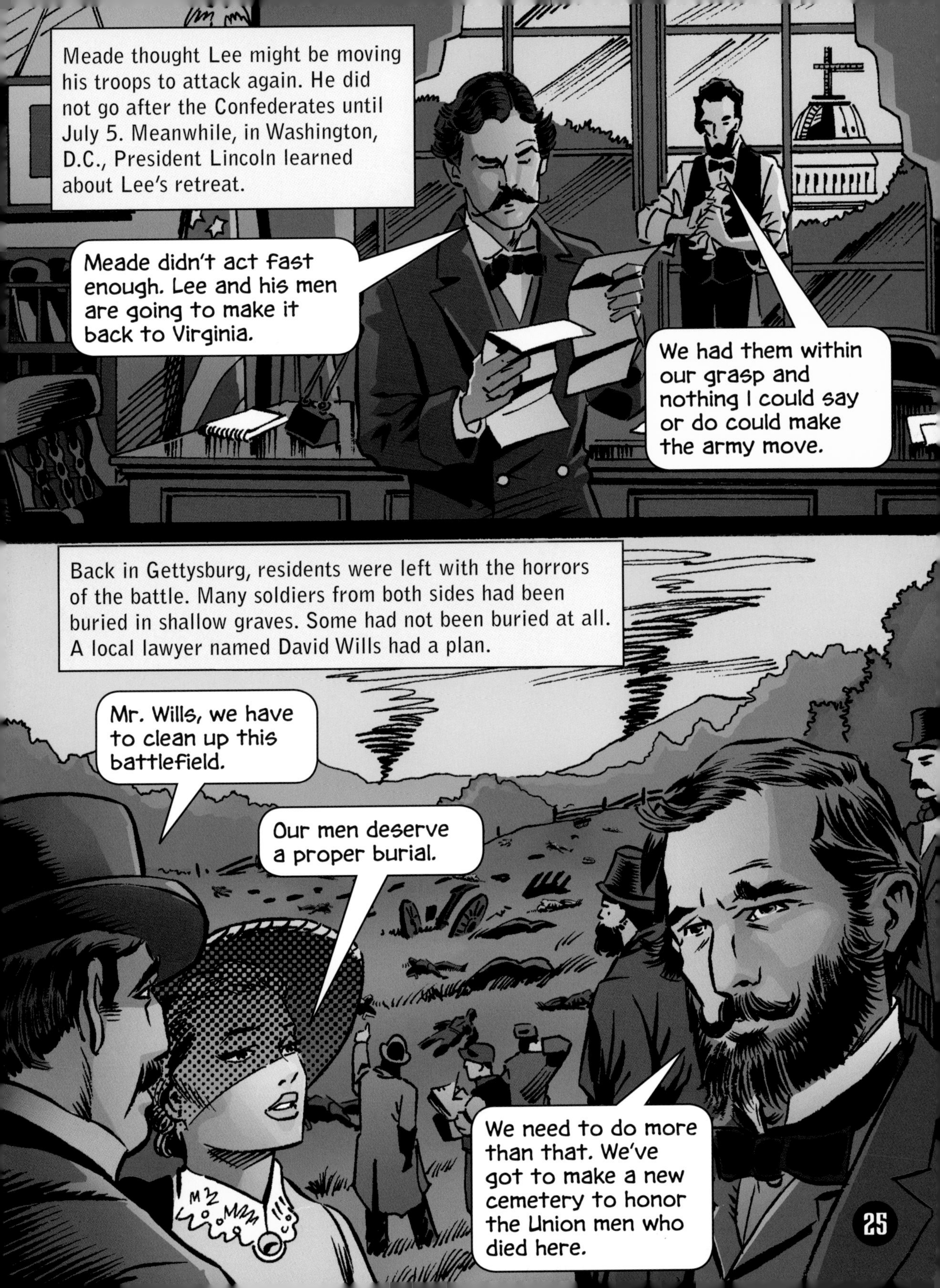
Meade thought Lee might be moving his troops to attack again. He did not go after the Confederates until July 5. Meanwhile, in Washington, D.C., President Lincoln learned about Lee's retreat.
Meade didn't act fast enough. Lee and his men are going to make it back to Virginia.
We had them within our grasp and nothing I could say or do could make the army move.
Back in Gettysburg, residents were left with the horrors of the battle. Many soldiers from both sides had been buried in shallow graves. Some had not been buried at all. A local lawyer named David Wills had a plan.
Mr. Wills, we have to clean up this battlefield.
Our men deserve a proper burial.
We need to do more than that. We've got to make a new cemetery to honor the Union men who died here.

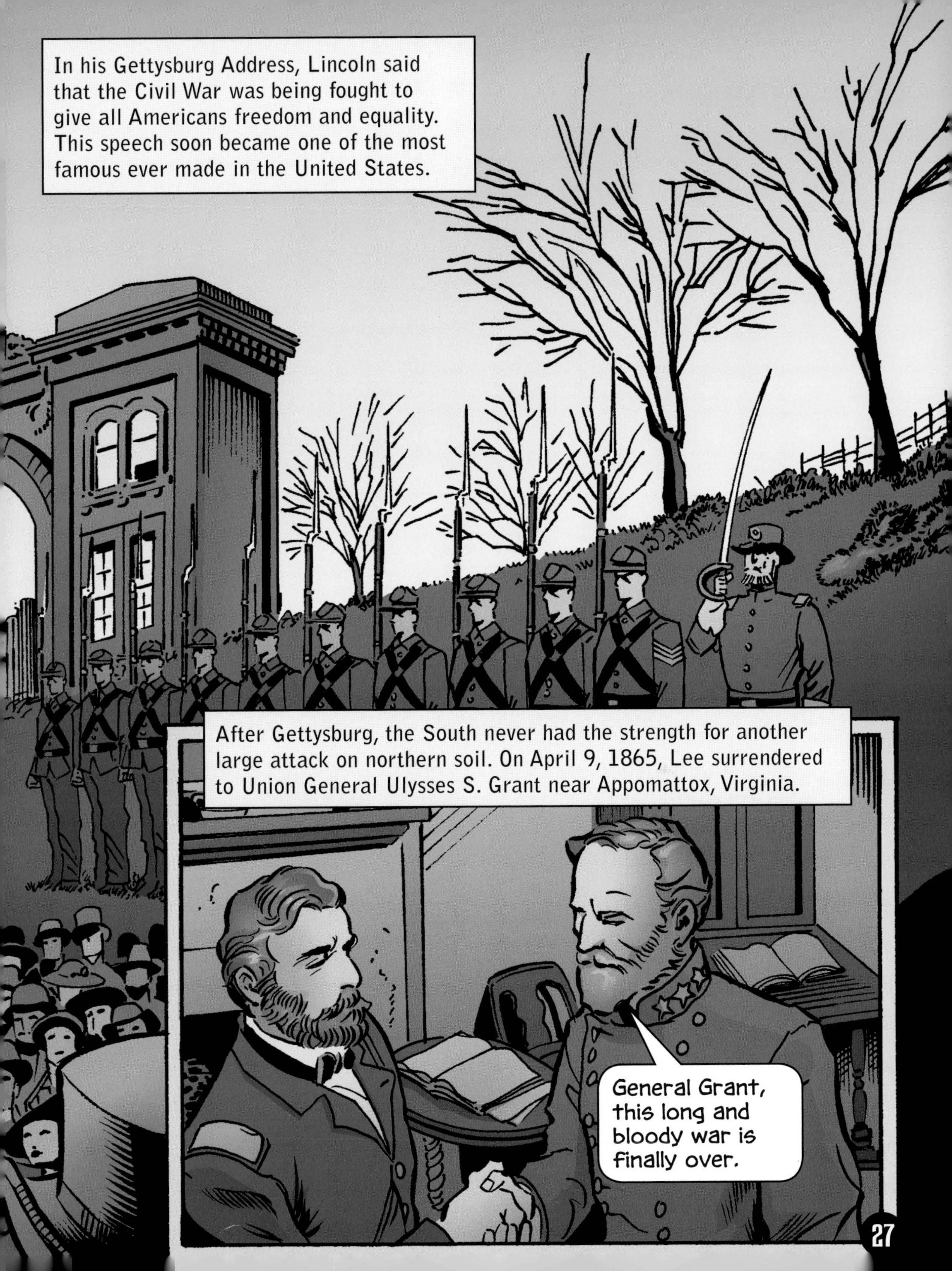
In his Gettysburg Address, Lincoln said that the Civil War was being fought to give all Americans freedom and equality. This speech soon became one of the most famous ever made in the United States.
After Gettysburg, the South never had the strength for another large attack on northern soil. On April 9, 1865, Lee surrendered to Union General Ulysses S. Grant near Appomattox, Virginia.
General Grant, this long and bloody war is finally over.

More about
The Battle of Gettysburg

 The North had about 22,000 casualties at Gettysburg, out of slightly more than 93,000 troops. The South suffered about the same number of casualties out of about 70,000 troops. The combined number of casualties was the highest for any one battle of the Civil War. About another 11,000 casualties occurred in the fighting just before and after the main battle.

 Abraham Lincoln personally wrote out five copies of the Gettysburg Address. Two are at the Library of Congress in Washington, D.C. One is in the White House and another is at the Abraham Lincoln Presidential Library in Springfield, Illinois. The last is at Cornell University in New York.

 About 3,500 Union soldiers are buried at the Soldiers' National Cemetery in Gettysburg.

 In 1895, the U.S. government created Gettysburg National Military Park. The park includes the cemetery and the battlefield around it. Today, the park covers nearly 6,000 acres and has 26 miles of roads. At least 1.8 million people visit the park each year.

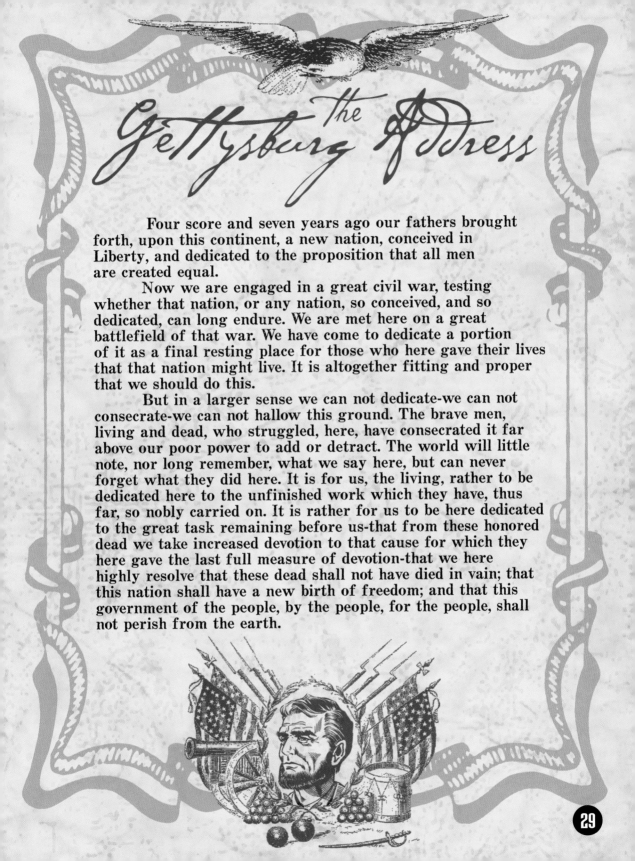

The Gettysburg Address

Four score and seven years ago our fathers brought forth, upon this continent, a new nation, conceived in Liberty, and dedicated to the proposition that all men are created equal.

Now we are engaged in a great civil war, testing whether that nation, or any nation, so conceived, and so dedicated, can long endure. We are met here on a great battlefield of that war. We have come to dedicate a portion of it as a final resting place for those who here gave their lives that that nation might live. It is altogether fitting and proper that we should do this.

But in a larger sense we can not dedicate-we can not consecrate-we can not hallow this ground. The brave men, living and dead, who struggled, here, have consecrated it far above our poor power to add or detract. The world will little note, nor long remember, what we say here, but can never forget what they did here. It is for us, the living, rather to be dedicated here to the unfinished work which they have, thus far, so nobly carried on. It is rather for us to be here dedicated to the great task remaining before us-that from these honored dead we take increased devotion to that cause for which they here gave the last full measure of devotion-that we here highly resolve that these dead shall not have died in vain; that this nation shall have a new birth of freedom; and that this government of the people, by the people, for the people, shall not perish from the earth.

GLOSSARY

ammunition (am-yuh-NISH-uhn)—bullets and other objects that can be fired from weapons; ammunition is called "ammo" for short.

artillery (ar-TIL-uh-ree)—large, powerful guns

casualties (KAZH-oo-uhl-tees)—soldiers killed, wounded, captured, or reported missing after a battle

corps (KOR)—a group of military officers and enlisted members

counterattack (KOUN-ter-uh-tak)—fighting begun by one side after it has slowed or stopped an enemy's original attack

flank (FLANGK)—area to the side of a group of soldiers

INTERNET SITES

FactHound offers a safe, fun way to find Internet sites related to this book. All of the sites on FactHound have been researched by our staff.

Here's how:

1. *Visit www.facthound.com*
2. Type in this special code **0736854916** for age-appropriate sites. Or enter a search word related to this book for a more general search.
3. Click on the **Fetch It** button.

FactHound will fetch the best sites for you!

READ MORE

Anderson, Dale. *The Battle of Gettysburg.* Landmark Events in American History. Milwaukee: World Almanac Library, 2003.

McPherson, James M. *Fields of Fury: The American Civil War.* New York: Atheneum Books for Young Readers, 2002.

Stone, Tanya Lee. *Abraham Lincoln.* DK Biography. New York: DK Publishing, 2005.

Tanaka, Shelley. *Gettysburg.* A Day that Changed America. New York: Hyperion Books for Children, 2003.

BIBLIOGRAPHY

Catton, Bruce. *The American Heritage New History of the Civil War.* New York: Viking, 1996.

Johnston, David Emmons. *The Story of a Confederate Boy in the Civil War.* Portland, Ore.: Glass & Prudhomme, 1914.

Sears, Stephen W. *Gettysburg.* Boston: Houghton Mifflin, 2003.

Tagg, Larry. *The Generals of Gettysburg: The Leaders of America's Greatest Battle.* Campbell, Calif.: Savas Publishing, 1998.

INDEX